Collins

INTERNATIONAL
PRIMARY
ENGLISH

Progress Book 6

Student's Book

William Collins' dream of knowledge for all began with the publication of his first book in 1819. A self-educated mill worker, he not only enriched millions of lives, but also founded a flourishing publishing house. Today, staying true to this spirit, Collins books are packed with inspiration, innovation and practical expertise. They place you at the centre of a world of possibility and give you exactly what you need to explore it.

Collins. Freedom to teach.

Published by Collins

An imprint of HarperCollins*Publishers*
The News Building, 1 London Bridge Street, London, SE1 9GF, UK

HarperCollins*Publishers*
Macken House, 39/40 Mayor Street Upper, Dublin 1, D01 C9W8, Ireland

Browse the complete Collins catalogue at
www.collins.co.uk

© HarperCollins*Publishers* Limited 2023

10 9 8 7 6 5 4 3 2 1

ISBN 978-0-00-865484-9

British Library Cataloguing-in-Publication Data
A catalogue record for this publication is available from the British Library.

Author: Fiona Macgregor
Series editor: Daphne Paizee
Publisher: Elaine Higgleton
Product manager: Holly Woolnough
Content editor: Daniela Mora Chavarría
Project manager: Just Content Ltd
Copy editor: Tanya Solomons
Proofreader: Catherine Dakin
Cover designer: Gordon MacGilp
Cover illustration: Nicholas Jackson
Typesetter: David Jimenez
Illustrator: Ann Paganuzzi
Production controller: Lyndsey Rogers
Printed and bound in Great Britain by Martins the Printers

With thanks to the following teachers for reviewing materials in proof and providing valuable feedback: Sylvie Meurein, Nilai International School; Gabriel Kehinde, Avi-Cenna International School; and with thanks to the following teachers who provided feedback during the early development stage: Najihah binti Roslan, Nilai International School.

MIX
Paper | Supporting
responsible forestry
FSC
www.fsc.org
FSC™ C007454

This book contains FSC™ certified paper and other controlled sources to ensure responsible forest management.

For more information visit: www.harpercollins.co.uk/green

The publishers gratefully acknowledge the permission granted to reproduce the copyright material in this book. Every effort has been made to trace copyright holders and to obtain their permission for the use of copyright material. The publishers will gladly receive any information enabling them to rectify any error or omission at the fi rst opportunity.

Cambridge International copyright material in this publication is reproduced under licence and remains the intellectual property of Cambridge Assessment International Education

This text has not been through the Cambridge International endorsement process.

Contents

How to use this book

This book is full of questions. Each set of questions can be completed at the end of each week.

The questions allow you to practise the things you've learned. They will help you understand topics that you might need more practice of. They will also show you the topics that you are most confident with. Your teacher can use your answers to give you feedback and support.

At the end of each set of questions, there is a space to put the date that you completed it. There is also a blank box. Your teacher might use it to:

- sign, when they have marked your answers

- write a short comment on your work.

Date: _____   Now look at and think about each of the *I can* statements.

Pages 5 to 11 include a list of *I can* statements. Once you have finished each set of questions, turn to the *I can* statements. Think about each statement: how easy or hard did you find the topic? For each statement, colour in the face that is closest to how you feel:

😊 I can do this   😐 I'm getting there   ☹ I need some help.

There are three longer termly tests in the book. These can be completed after each block of units.

Answers and audio files for each test are available by request from www.collins.co.uk/internationalresources.

I can statements

At the end of each unit, think about each of the *I can* statements and how easy or hard you find the topic. For each statement, colour in the face that is closest to how you feel.

Unit 1 Backwards and forwards	Date:		
Week 1			
I can listen to and read different fiction genres.	🙂	😐	🙁
I can identify features of texts.	🙂	😐	🙁
I can find and use interesting words in a text.	🙂	😐	🙁
Week 2			
I can change adjectives to nouns.	🙂	😐	🙁
I can use the active and passive voice.	🙂	😐	🙁
I can use punctuation marks to add emphasis.	🙂	😐	🙁
Week 3			
I can plan, draft, proofread and edit my writing.	🙂	😐	🙁
I can identify the features of a newspaper report.	🙂	😐	🙁
I can write a newspaper report.	🙂	😐	🙁
Unit 2 Family matters	**Date:**		
Week 1			
I can read and enjoy a playscript and a news report.	🙂	😐	🙁
I can answer questions with reference to the text.	🙂	😐	🙁
I can identify rhyming words.	🙂	😐	🙁

Week 2			
I can use brackets correctly.	☺	😐	☹
I can use interesting adverbs and adjectives.	☺	😐	☹
I can identify synonyms and antonyms.	☺	😐	☹
Week 3			
I can rewrite a poem into a playscript.	☺	😐	☹
I can use language to make my characters interesting.	☺	😐	☹
Unit 3 From pencils to pixels	**Date:**		
Week 1			
I can read an autobiography/biography and respond personally.	☺	😐	☹
I can identify different narrative points of view.	☺	😐	☹
I can identify nouns and understand their purpose.	☺	😐	☹
Week 2			
I can spell and punctuate correctly.	☺	😐	☹
I can use adjectives.	☺	😐	☹
I can transform meaning with suffixes.	☺	😐	☹
I can use apostrophes correctly.	☺	😐	☹
Week 3			
I can explore the use of words from other languages.	☺	😐	☹
I can plan and write an autobiographical account.	☺	😐	☹

Term 1 Test			
I can identify different types of text.	☺	😐	☹
I can identify parts of speech.	☺	😐	☹
I can punctuate correctly.	☺	😐	☹
I can continue a piece of writing in a particular genre.	☺	😐	☹

Unit 4 It's about time	Date:		
Week 1			
I can identify fiction and non-fiction text.	☺	😐	☹
I can recognise the features of a fiction text.	☺	😐	☹
I can use direct and indirect speech.	☺	😐	☹
Week 2			
I can structure simple sentences.	☺	😐	☹
I can use relative pronouns in sentences.	☺	😐	☹
I can use suffixes to change verbs to nouns.	☺	😐	☹
I can identify figurative language.	☺	😐	☹
Week 3			
I can use figurative language.	☺	😐	☹
I can plan, structure and plot a story.	☺	😐	☹

Unit 5 Facts and fables	Date:		
Week 1			
I can identify the features of information texts.	☺	😐	☹
I can use language to convey my ideas and opinions.	☺	😐	☹
I can use simple, compound and complex sentences.	☺	😐	☹
Week 2			
I can identify and use figurative language.	☺	😐	☹
I can learn spelling rules around the 'k' sound.	☺	😐	☹
I can write a short, interesting fable.	☺	😐	☹
Week 3			
I can use a variety of sentence types to make my writing interesting.	☺	😐	☹
I can plan, structure and write a report.	☺	😐	☹
Unit 6 Holey-moley!	Date:		
Week 1			
I can tell the difference between fact and opinion.	☺	😐	☹
I can infer implicit and explicit meanings in a text.	☺	😐	☹
I can use connectives to sequence events.	☺	😐	☹
Week 2			
I can make notes for a speech.	☺	😐	☹
I can link ideas using connectives.	☺	😐	☹
I can use prefixes to create opposites.	☺	😐	☹
I can explore spelling rules and exceptions.	☺	😐	☹

Week 3			
I can write a Kennings.	☺	😐	☹
I can write a story with a flashback.	☺	😐	☹
Term 2 Test			
I can answer questions about a text in different genres.	☺	😐	☹
I can write an information text.	☺	😐	☹
Unit 7 Stop!	**Date:**		
Week 1			
I can recognise persuasive language.	☺	😐	☹
I can identify shades of meaning in the use of words and phrases.	☺	😐	☹
Week 2			
I can use colons and semicolons.	☺	😐	☹
I can use action verbs and linking verbs.	☺	😐	☹
I can spell words with the 'j' sound.	☺	😐	☹
Week 3			
I can plan a persuasive argument.	☺	😐	☹
I can write an essay with a balanced argument.	☺	😐	☹

Unit 8 I spy	Date:		
Week 1			
I can read and respond to a biography and an infographic.	😊	😐	☹️
I can scan a text to identify its features.	😊	😐	☹️
I can draw an infographic.	😊	😐	☹️
I can use verb forms appropriately.	😊	😐	☹️
Week 2			
I can add prefixes to root words to transform their meaning.	😊	😐	☹️
I can use the active and passive voice.	😊	😐	☹️
I can use verb forms correctly.	😊	😐	☹️
I can use the conventions of standard English (spelling and punctuation).	😊	😐	☹️
Week 3			
I can create an infographic.	😊	😐	☹️
I can write a letter/an email.	😊	😐	☹️
Unit 9 Star-crossed	Date:		
Week 1			
I can listen, read and respond to a playscript.	😊	😐	☹️
I can use language to convey ideas and opinions.	😊	😐	☹️
I can understand figurative language.	😊	😐	☹️

Week 2			
I can use verb forms accurately.	☺	😐	☹
I can write complex sentences.	☺	😐	☹
I can use a wide range of words and figurative language.	☺	😐	☹
Week 3			
I can write a playscript.	☺	😐	☹
I can read aloud fluently.	☺	😐	☹
I can write a review.	☺	😐	☹
Term 3 Test			
I can summarise a text.	☺	😐	☹
I can respond to a poem.	☺	😐	☹
I can identify features of a piece of writing.	☺	😐	☹
I can use different sentence constructions.	☺	😐	☹
I can write a persuasive text.	☺	😐	☹

1 🎧 Audio 1 Listen to this extract from *The Railway Children*, then answer the questions.

They weren't railway children to begin with. They were just ordinary children, and they lived with their father and mother in a large redbrick house in the suburbs of London. There were three of them. The eldest was Roberta – Bobbie for short. Next came Peter, and the youngest was Phyllis.

These three lucky children had everything they needed: good clothes, warm fires and plenty of toys, a mother who made up funny pieces of poetry for their birthdays, and a father who was never cross, never unjust and always ready for a game.

They ought to have been very happy. And so they were, but they didn't know *how* happy until their life in the redbrick house was over and done with, and they had to live a very different life indeed.

The dreadful change came quite suddenly. … After dinner … there was a knock on the front door. A moment later the maid came in and said that two gentlemen wanted to see Father.

"Get rid of them quickly, dear, whoever they are," said Mother, as Father got out of his chair. "It's nearly the children's bedtime."

But Father couldn't get rid of them quickly. Peter, Bobbie and Phyllis waited a long time. They could hear Father talking to the gentlemen in another room, and his voice sounded louder than usual and different, somehow. After a while Mother went to join them, and there was more talking.

At last the children heard boots go out and down the front steps. "They're leaving!" said Phyllis with relief. The *clip-clop* of hooves echoed in the street outside as a horse-drawn cab drove away.

Then Mother came back into the room. Her face was as white as her lace collar, and her eyes looked very big and shining.

"Father's been called away – on business," she said. "Come, darlings, it's your bedtime."

The next morning, when the children came down to breakfast, Mother had already gone out. It was seven in the evening before she got back, looking so ill and tired that the children felt they couldn't ask her any questions. She sank into an armchair and Peter fetched her soft velvety slippers.

Then one morning, at breakfast, Mother said, "Everything's settled, my pets. We're going to leave this house, and go and live in the country."

a Where did the children live at the beginning of the story?

_____

b How do we know, from the beginning, that there will be a change in their lives?

_____

c Why did the narrator consider the children 'lucky'? Tick (✓) one answer.

☐ They lived in London.

☐ They had everything they needed.

☐ They had a railway line near them.

d What is the first change in the lives of the children?

_____

e What is the second change, on page 13?

_____

f Why do you think the mother chose the plainest furniture to take with them?

_____

g Why does she say, "We've got to play at being poor for a bit." Tick (✓) one answer.

☐ They are in a play about being poor.

☐ She wants to make being poor seem like a game.

☐ They are playing a game.

h Where do you think the children will end up living?

_____

i Explain your answer to part **h**.

_____

2 Read this extract from *Hall of the Bulls*, then answer the questions.

Chapter 1

The cave was dark as Simon and Dan squeezed through the passage. Cold water dripped on them from above and the air smelt of mould. The only light came from the weak torches strapped to their foreheads. They came out into a big chamber and gathered round the tour guide. "This is the most famous painting in the caves," said the tour guide, pointing at a huge picture on the wall. "The Great Bull!" For the first time during the tour, Class 4C was quiet. Everyone had been having a lot of fun on the school trip to France. That usually meant noise – laughing, talking and shouting. Now, the students were impressed and listened carefully.

Chapter 2

"That's strange, the paintings look clearer …" Simon said, frowning. The paintings looked as though they had just been painted – the colours were bright and strong, and the bulls loomed out of the darkness at them. The cave suddenly felt cold and spooky.

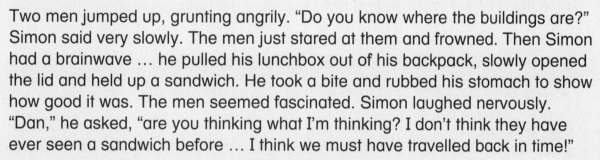

When they got outside, they couldn't believe their eyes. The building where they'd met the guide had disappeared. And they were completely alone. All they could see were trees – a forest had replaced the buildings. The boys walked towards a line of smoke rising above the trees and found some people sitting around a fire, wearing strange clothes, fur and bits of leather.

Two men jumped up, grunting angrily. "Do you know where the buildings are?" Simon said very slowly. The men just stared at them and frowned. Then Simon had a brainwave … he pulled his lunchbox out of his backpack, slowly opened the lid and held up a sandwich. He took a bite and rubbed his stomach to show how good it was. The men seemed fascinated. Simon laughed nervously. "Dan," he asked, "are you thinking what I'm thinking? I don't think they have ever seen a sandwich before … I think we must have travelled back in time!"

a Where are the children as Chapter 1 opens?

_____

b What is the sudden change in Chapter 2?

_____

c Write a sentence from Chapter 2 to show what the boys think caused this change.

_____

d Write three of your own interesting adjectives to describe the people the boys encounter.

_____

e Write three verbs from the text to show how the people communicated with the boys.

_____

3 Read this extract from Chapter 3 of *Hall of the Bulls*, then answer the questions.

Chapter 3

As they got nearer the caves, a great roaring sound was heard. Everyone stopped. Soon they knew what was making the noise – a giant bull was standing in front of the cave and it looked angry. It roared and charged at them. Its hooves sounded like thunder as they hit the ground. The boys ran back into the trees as fast as they could. The animal only stopped when it couldn't see them anymore. After what felt like a century, Dan had an idea. He took out his lunchbox, took out an apple and threw it to the animal. Carefully the children inched around the bull and hurried back to the cave. It was pitch black and the cavemen kids were amazed when Simon and Dan switched on their torches and the cave was suddenly lighter.

---

a Fill in the missing action verbs in this sentence.

It _____ and _____ at them.

b Write a simile from the text that describes the bull.

_____

c Rewrite this sentence, correcting all the errors.

The boys run back in to the trees so fast as thay could.

_____

d Underline the verbs in this sentence. Then replace them with more interesting action verbs.

The children walked around the bull and went back to the cave.

_____

_____

e Write this sentence in direct speech. Remember to punctuate it correctly.

He said that they must have been away for ages, but that it felt like only a few minutes.

_____

_____

_____

4 What are the features of a story?

a Look at the words in the box. Choose the ones about a story. Fill in a flowchart, like this one, with the features of a story.

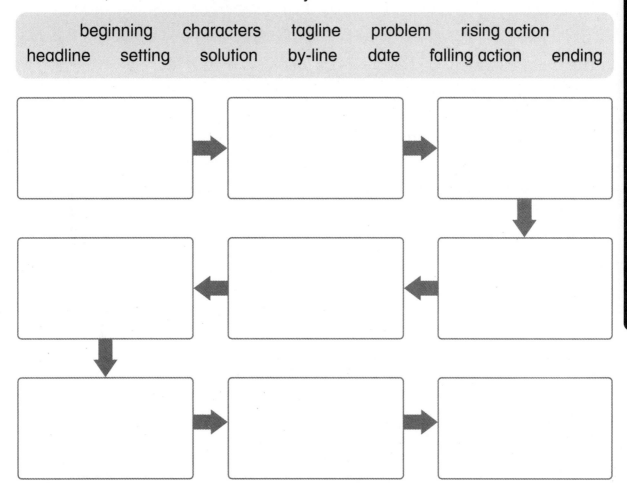

| beginning | characters | tagline | problem | rising action |
| headline | setting | solution | by-line | date | falling action | ending |

b Identify the features of *Hall of the Bulls*, using your flowchart.

_____

_____

_____

_____

_____

_____

_____

_____

Look at and think about each of the *I can* statements.

Date: _____

1 Read this text, then answer the questions.

> She stared at the <u>elegant</u> display of objects that had been found in the ruins.
> An <u>important</u>-looking notice said: Touching the exhibits is forbidden.
>
> "Goodness," she thought to herself. "Why do they even need to say that in a museum?"
>
> There was a sudden, loud crash. Glass splintered around her, then everything went dark. A hand moved quickly past her and grabbed the emerald statue and the glittering diamond bracelet.
>
> "Ouch!" she cried. "You <u>arrogant</u>, <u>ignorant</u> idiot!"
>
> The alarm button was pressed and she was surrounded by a piercing, brain-deadening screech.

a What type of text is this? Tick (✓) one answer.

☐ factual information   ☐ fiction   ☐ a newspaper report

b Give a reason for your answer to part **a**.

_____

c Describe the setting of this piece of writing.

_____

d Write four short sentences describing the action that takes place.

_____

_____

_____

e Change the underlined adjectives in the text into nouns.

_____

_____

2 Read the text again.

a Find and write two examples of the passive voice from the text.

_____

_____

b Use your own punctuation to make these sentences more interesting.

There was a sudden, loud crash. Glass splintered around her, then everything went dark.

_____

_____

c Rewrite this sentence in indirect speech.

"Goodness," she thought to herself. "Why do they even need to say that in a museum?"

_____

_____

d Which adjectives in this text do you find interesting? Choose two and write them in sentences of your own.

_____

_____

e Complete this sentence with a strong action verb of your choice.

"Ouch!" she _____.

3 Change these sentences into the active voice.

a The event was watched by thousands of people.

_____

b The town was covered in ash and flaming debris.

_____

c A letter describing the eruption was found by archaeologists.

_____

d The exhibition was organised by the curator.

_____

4 Change these sentences into the passive voice.

a We all attended the exhibition.

_____

b The boys ignored the display of household objects.

_____

c They caused a lot of trouble.

_____

d Obey the rules!

_____

Look at and think about each of the *I can* statements.

Date: _____

1 Write a newspaper report based on one of the stories that you read in Chapter 1, or on the paragraphs in Week 2.

a First, revise the features of a newspaper report.

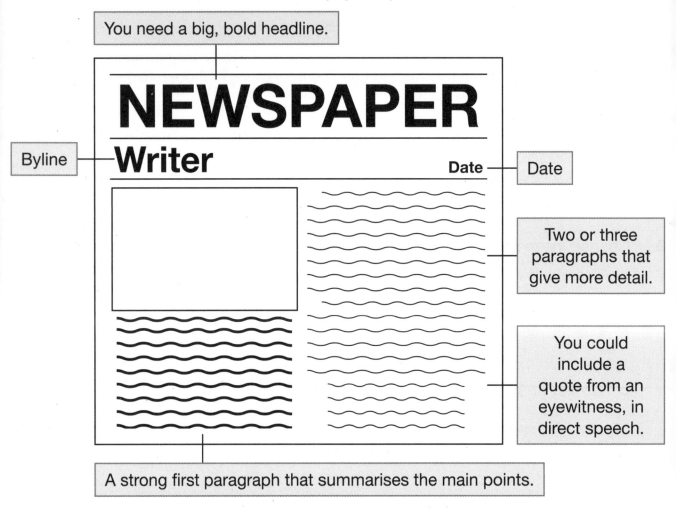

You need a big, bold headline.

NEWSPAPER

Byline — **Writer**

Date — Date

Two or three paragraphs that give more detail.

You could include a quote from an eyewitness, in direct speech.

A strong first paragraph that summarises the main points.

b Make rough notes about what you would like to write about in the space below. You could use a mind map to help you.

c Check that your plan includes all the features of a newspaper report.

d If you like, swap your notes with a friend and check each other's work. Make kind, constructive suggestions for improving their writing.

2   Write your report out neatly here.

_____

_____

_____

_____

_____

_____

_____

_____

_____

_____

_____

_____

_____

_____

_____

_____

_____

_____

_____

_____

_____

_____

_____

_____

Unit 1 Backwards and forwards

Look at and think about each of the *I can* statements.

Date: _____

1 Read the beginning of the play, *The Porridge Pincher*, by David Wood, then answer the questions.

The Porridge Pincher

(Enter the Storyteller.)

Storyteller:	Down in the country, deep in the wood. Is a cottage where once an oak tree stood. Living inside is a family:

(Enter the Three Bears.)

Father Bear:	Father!
Mother Bear:	Mother!
Baby Bear:	And baby, that's me!
Storyteller:	Nobody goes there unawares. For this is the home of …
Bears:	Three brown bears!
Mother Bear:	Time to get up!
Storyteller:	Cries mother one morning
Mother Bear:	Rise and shine Baby Bear stop your yawning. Daddy's cooking breakfast
Father Bear:	Eggs or toast?
Baby Bear:	What I fancy most is porridge, Daddy, porridge please
Mother Bear:	That sounds tasty
Storyteller:	Mum agrees. So using all his cooking skills Father heats and stirs and fills Three steaming bowls, but then, guess what? They taste it and …
Bears:	It's far too hot!
Father Bear:	Never mind,
Storyteller:	Smiles Dad.
Father Bear:	Don't fret, don't frown. We'll go for a walk till the porridge cools down.

(Exit Three Bears. Enter Goldilocks.)

---

a Who, or what, is 'The Porridge Pincher'?

_____

b Find a line that means the same as 'people don't go there on purpose'.

_____

c What do you think is going to happen next in this play?

_____

d What features of this text tell you that it is a play?

_____

_____

e What is the function of the words in brackets?

_____

f Read the play aloud. Write the words that rhyme.

_____

_____

g Which rhyming lines work the best, in your opinion? Write them out and explain why you think so.

_____

_____

_____

h Are there lines that don't rhyme as well? Write them out and explain why you think so.

_____

_____

_____

i Choose two rhyming words and write your own rhyming couplet.

_____

_____

2   Draw lines to match each word to its meaning.

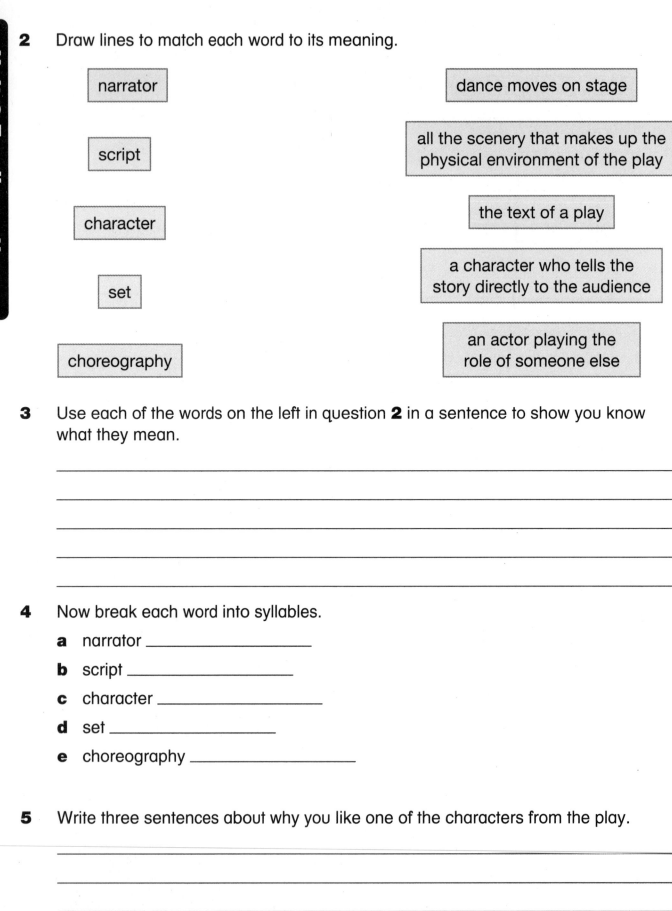

narrator

script

character

set

choreography

dance moves on stage

all the scenery that makes up the physical environment of the play

the text of a play

a character who tells the story directly to the audience

an actor playing the role of someone else

3   Use each of the words on the left in question **2** in a sentence to show you know what they mean.

_____

_____

_____

_____

_____

4   Now break each word into syllables.

a   narrator _____

b   script _____

c   character _____

d   set _____

e   choreography _____

5   Write three sentences about why you like one of the characters from the play.

_____

_____

_____

_____

6 Read this news report, then answer the questions.

'Bear-ly' burgled!

by F Macgregor

London

An intruder <u>broke into</u> the Bear home, ate their food, destroyed their furniture, and was found asleep in one of their beds.

This morning the Bear family came home to a shocking sight. An intruder had broken into their house. The suspect was found fast asleep in the children's room after eating the family's breakfast, and apparently reducing a wooden chair to matchsticks. "It was very <u>traumatic</u>," said Mrs Bear.

The <u>intruder</u> was taken to the police station in handcuffs. Her name has not been released to the press, but a witness described her as "a slight person, with blonde hair, wearing a pink cardigan. She looked suspicious."

More information will follow. Our reporter is attending the hearing tomorrow.

a Explain the pun in the headline.

_____

b The writer uses emotive words to get a response from the reader. Find three emotive words in paragraph 2.

_____

c How do these words make you feel?

_____

d Write an example of over-exaggeration in the news report.

_____

e Find synonyms for the underlined words to make this report less emotive.

_____

f Based on the information in the news report, write three sentences about the character of the 'intruder'.

_____

_____

_____

Look at and think about each of the *I can* statements.

Date: _____

1 Rewrite these sentences. Add the missing brackets.

a They arrested the woman the one in the pink cardigan and took her to the police station.

_____

_____

b Brackets also called parentheses are used to add extra information to a sentence.

_____

_____

c You can delete the words the extra ones I mean and the sentence will still make sense.

_____

_____

d Character traits are words descriptive ones like adjectives that tell us more about a character.

_____

_____

e That family the one that lives in the woods had a break-in.

_____

2 Imagine you went to see a play. Add adverbs to these paragraphs to make them more interesting.

_____ we went to see a play. We were a bit late, so we parked _____ and had to run to get there _____.
The audience applauded _____ when we walked in, which was _____ embarrassing! We waited _____ for the curtains to open.

The show was fantastic. We clapped _____ at the end.
There is another performance _____. I might come and watch it _____. Look out for the review in the paper _____.

3 Use interesting adjectives to describe what the person in this photograph looks like. Write at least three sentences.

_____

_____

_____

_____

_____

_____

_____

4 Now describe what you think the person does, in three sentences, using interesting adverbs.

_____

_____

_____

_____

_____

_____

5 Write synonyms and antonyms for these character traits.

Character trait	synonym	antonym
a caring		
b bad-tempered		
c mature		
d childish		
e strange		
f cruel		

Look at and think about each of the _I can_ statements.

Date: _____

1 Read the poem 'Gran, can you rap?' again.

> ## Gran, can you rap? *by Jack Ousbey*
>
> Gran was in her chair she was taking a nap
> When I tapped her on the shoulder to see if she could rap.
> Gran, can you rap? Can you rap? Can you, Gran?
> And she opened one eye and she said to me, "Man,
> I'm the best rapping Gran this world's ever seen
> I'm a tip-top, slip-slap, rap-rap queen."
>
> And she rose from her chair in the corner of the room
> And she started to rap with a bim-bam-boom,
> And she rolled up her eyes and she rolled round her head
> And as she rolled by this is what she said,
> "I'm the best rapping Gran this world's ever seen
> I'm a nip-nap, yip-yap, rap-rap queen."
>
> Then she rapped past my dad and she rapped past my mother,
> She rapped past me and my little baby brother.
> She rapped her arms narrow she rapped her arms wide,
> She rapped through the door and she rapped outside.
> She's the best rapping Gran this world's ever seen
> She's a drip-drop, trip-trap, rap-rap queen.

You are going to use the poem to write a playscript featuring Gran, the boy or girl, and one other character of your choice.

a Start by making notes about your three characters. What do they look like? How do they behave?

_____

_____

_____

b Now make notes of the setting so that you can write stage directions. Where are they? What is around them? What's the weather like?

_____

_____

_____

c Finally, write a few short sentences about what is going to happen in your script.

_____

_____

2 It's time to write your script. Use your notes to help you.

_____

_____

_____

_____

_____

_____

_____

_____

_____

_____

_____

_____

_____

_____

_____

_____

_____

_____

3 Use this checklist to improve and edit your text.

Checklist

- Have you got clear stage directions in brackets? ☐

- Does your writing use the playscript format? ☐

- Have you used interesting adjectives and adverbs? ☐

- Have you checked your spelling and punctuation? ☐

Look at and think about each of the _I can_ statements. ☐

Date: _____

1 Read this extract from Michael Rosen's book, *All about me*, then answer the questions.

From the age of about seven, Harrybo was my main pal. He lived at the end of my road and we just hung out together all the time.

Sometimes we'd explore the countryside – the woods, the farm and the river Pinn, which we would walk along for miles. We'd spend hours playing with the stuff people used to throw into the river, like old bikes and prams. Or we'd go 'ponding' and try to catch tadpoles, newts and frogs.

Sometimes we'd go towards the 'towny' bit, which is called Wealdstone and Harrow, and go to the swimming baths and the chip shop, and hang about in the streets.

There were two guys who used to stand outside Harrow and Wealdstone station selling newspapers – a great big bloke and a little tiny bloke – and the great big bloke used to say, "Nah new an nan nah," which actually meant "Star, News and Standard".

These were the names of the three newspapers he was selling, but you couldn't really tell. Then the little bloke next to him would say, in a deep gruff voice, "Ay ah!" and that meant "Late Star". So they'd stand there outside the station, taking it in turns to say their words. Harrybo and I thought this was hysterically funny, so we used to stand on the other side of the road and imitate them: "Nah new an nan nah," and "Ay ah!" Of course we got chased off.

Harrybo and I read books at the same time and then talked about them. After reading the two Winnie the Pooh books, I can remember we walked along the road together singing, "My nose is cold-tiddley-pom."

a What type of text is this? Tick (✓) one answer.

☐ a biography　　　☐ a story　　　☐ an autobiography

b Give a reason for your answer to part **a**.

_____

c From whose point of view is this extract written?

_____

d Write these phrases using more formal language.

i my main pal

_____

ii we just hung out together

_____

iii the stuff people used to throw in the river

_____

iv the 'towny' bit

_____

e What are The Star, News and Standard?

_____

f What types of noun are these?

i Harrybo _____

ii the woods, the farm and the river _____

iii Wealdstone _____

g Find three adjectives in this phrase.

Then the little bloke next to him would say, in a deep gruff voice ...

_____

h What was the 'great big bloke' saying when he said, "Nah new an nan nah"?

_____

i How did the little bloke say 'Late Star'?

_____

j Why do you think Michael Rosen spelled the men's words like he did?

_____

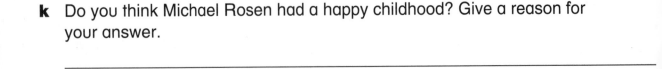

k Do you think Michael Rosen had a happy childhood? Give a reason for your answer.

_____

_____

2 Read this text, then answer the questions.

> They grew up in an orphanage. It was not an unhappy time, exactly, just not a happy one. James only came to recognise that as an adult, once he had experienced true happiness.
>
> They had food and clothes and, if not parents, then at least they had each other. There was a girls' dormitory and a boys' one. Each child had a locker where they could keep precious things. James's locker was full of rocks, and interesting things that he found on his nature walks. Sessie had very few precious treasures – an eye make-up kit which was her mother's, a piece of lace from a childhood dress, and a charm bracelet, from her first birthday, which she didn't remember at all.

a Is this a first-person or a third-person narrator?

_____

b What is the function of a narrator in a text?

_____

c Who do you think will be the main character in this story?

_____

d How did James feel when he was growing up?

_____

e Write two adjectives from the first paragraph.

_____

f Find an abstract noun that is made from the adjective 'happy'.

_____

g What is the function of the two apostrophes in this phrase?

There was a girls' dormitory and a boys' one.

_____

h How would the meaning change if the sentence said, 'There was a girl's dormitory and a boy's one.'?

_____

i Find a sentence in the text that shows what James was interested in.

_____

j What does the collection in Sessie's locker say about her?

_____

3 Write **fewer** or **less** to complete each sentence.

a Sessie had _____ treasures in her locker than James.

b Michael paid _____ attention to his work than he should have.

c We have _____ water in our rainwater tank than last year.

d They had _____ fun at the orphanage than at school.

e We can hear _____ voices now that the teacher has arrived.

4 Make nouns of career names from the words in the box. Then write a sentence for each word to show that you know what it means.

| optic | magic | electric | music |

_____

_____

_____

_____

_____

5 Write your own collective nouns for these phrases, then use each in a sentence.

a _____ of happy children

a _____ of newspapers

a _____ of rocks and leaves

_____

_____

_____

_____

_____

Date: _____

Look at and think about each of the _I can_ statements.

1 Imagine that James, from the orphanage, wrote a letter to his friend Harry. Correct any errors that you find by writing the corrections on the letter itself.

Dear Harry

Thanks for the parcel. It was very heavy. Ill add the rocks to my collection. We were more interested in the cakes they were delishous. My friends dont have pals like you so I shared not the rocks the cakes.

Were having a problem here with our one teacher miss ogeny. Shes young but im quiet scared of her. One move and your in detention.

Thanks for you're offer to come and stay for the weekend. id love to. Itll be such fun. Im happy to help with chores etc if you need a hand.

See you soon!
You're friend
James

2 Use the adjectives from the box to complete these sentences.

| local | their | evening | hysterically | English |

a Michael bought an _____ newspaper.

b They swam in the _____ river

c They took it in turns to say _____ words.

d The two boys thought it was _____ funny.

e They loved reading _____ books, like *Winnie the Pooh*.

3 For each adjective in question **2**, write whether it is **descriptive**, **proper** or **possessive**.

local   their   evening

_____   _____   _____

hysterically   English

_____   _____

4 Change the words in the table into nouns. Underline the suffixes.

a	educate	
b	loyal	
c	sad	
d	protect	
e	brave	

5 Rewrite these sentences. Change the underlined words to contractions.

a We <u>will not</u> give up our dream. _____

b It <u>is not</u> easy for children everywhere to receive an education. _____

c <u>We would</u> spend hours playing in the ponds. _____

d You <u>could not</u> really tell what he was talking about. _____

e She <u>did not</u> stop; she jumped right in to help. _____

Look at and think about each of the *I can* statements.

Date: _____

1   Find out where three of the words in the box come from.

ketchup   loot   cartoon   guru   safari   fiesta

a   Write a short description of what each word means in its original language.

b   Then explain why you think the word was 'borrowed' in English.

1 _____

_____

2 _____

_____

3 _____

_____

2   Write an autobiographical blog about something that happened to you that made a big impression on you.

• It could be something at school,

• or something that happened at home,

• or you could make up something, if you prefer.

You should write at least four paragraphs.

a   First, make rough notes about the event. Use words like *first*, *then*, *next* and *finally* to join your paragraphs.

_____

_____

_____

_____

_____

_____

_____

_____

_____

_____

_____

_____

b   Give your blog a title.

c   Swap your notes with a friend and see if you can help each other with constructive suggestions for improvements.

d Now, write your autobiographical blog out neatly.

_____

_____

_____

_____

_____

_____

_____

_____

_____

_____

_____

_____

_____

_____

_____

_____

_____

_____

Unit 3 From pencils to pixels

e Use this checklist to edit and improve your writing.

Checklist

- Does your blog have a catchy title? ☐

- Have you written in the first person (I, me)? ☐

- Have you checked your sentence structure? ☐

- Did you use some interesting adjectives? ☐

- Have you checked your spelling and punctuation? ☐

- Is your blog interesting, so the reader is captivated? ☐

Look at and think about each of the *I can* statements. ☐

Date: _____

1 Reading

Read the text from *I am Malala*, by Malala Yousafzai, then answer the questions.

I come from a country which was created at midnight. When I almost died, it was just after midday.

One year ago I left my home for school and never returned. I was shot in the head and I was flown out of Pakistan unconscious. Some people say I will never return home but I believe firmly in my heart that I will. To be torn from the country that you love is not something to wish on anyone.

Now, every morning when I open my eyes, I long to see my old room full of my things, my clothes all over the floor and my school prizes on the shelves. Instead I am in a country which is five hours behind my beloved Pakistan and my home in the Swat Valley. But my country is centuries behind this one. Here there is any convenience you can imagine. Water running from every tap, hot or cold as you wish; lights at the flick of a switch, day and night, no need for oil lamps; ovens to cook on that don't need anyone to fetch gas cylinders from the bazaar. Here everything is so modern one can even find food ready cooked in packets.

When I stand in front of my window and look out, I see tall buildings, long roads full of vehicles moving in orderly lines, neat green hedges and lawns, and tidy pavements to walk on. I close my eyes and for a moment I am back in my valley – the high snow-topped mountains, green waving fields and fresh blue rivers – and my heart smiles when it looks at the people of Swat. My mind transports me back to my school and there I am reunited with my friends and teachers. I meet my best friend Moniba and we sit together, talking and joking as if I had never left.

Then I remember I am in Birmingham, England.

a What type of text is this? Tick (✓) one answer.

☐ biography ☐ autobiography ☐ story ☐ news report

b Explain your answer to part **a**.

_____

c What would the writer not wish on anyone? [paragraph 2]

_____

d Identify an adverb of manner in this sentence.

I believe firmly in my heart that I will.

_____

e What three things does the writer long to see when she wakes up in the morning?

_____

_____

_____

f Write a proper noun and a common noun from paragraph 3.

_____

g The writer says her country is 'centuries behind this one'. Find three examples that she gives for thinking this.

_____

_____

_____

h The contrast in paragraph 4 is between:

☐ the city and the countryside   ☐ the colours blue and green

☐ the writer's home and where she is now.

i Quote a line that proves the writer was happy in her home town.

_____

j Find synonyms for these words from the last paragraph.

orderly _____   fresh _____

reunited _____

2 Grammar

a Name the underlined parts of speech in the text below. Write your answers in the table.

> The day when everything <u>changed</u> was <u>Tuesday</u>, 9 October 2012. It wasn't the best of days to start with, as it was the middle of <u>school</u> exams, though as a bookish girl I didn't mind them as much as some of <u>my</u> classmates.

Word from text	Part of speech
changed	
Tuesday	
school	
my	

b Find two uses of the apostrophe in the text above. Write the words out in full.

_____

c Rewrite these sentences using the correct punctuation.

    i The three girls books were on the table.

    _____

    ii Space travel is so exciting it is also dangerous

    _____

    iii "I don't think they've seen a sandwich before I think we must have time travelled."

    _____

    iv The girl the one I told you about yesterday is sitting right over there!

    _____

d Look at the photograph, then answer the questions.

    i Write a sentence about the picture in the active voice.

    _____

    ii Write a sentence about the picture in the passive voice.

    _____

    iii Write an opinion about the picture.

    _____

    iv Write a fact about the picture.

    _____

e Change these words into nouns.

    i peaceful _____   **ii** kind _____

    iii satisfy _____   **iv** reject _____.

3 Writing

a Continue the autobiographical story from question **1**.

You should consider:

- what the writer likes and doesn't like
- where she is
- what she believes
- what might happen next.

You do not have to complete the story. Write at least four paragraphs about something that happens next, from the writer's point of view.

b Plan your writing here.

_____

_____

_____

_____

_____

_____

c Write your story here.

_____

_____

_____

_____

_____

_____

_____

_____

_____

_____

_____

_____

_____

Look at and think about each of the *I can* statements.

Date: _____

1 Read this extract from *The Cosmic Laundry Basket*, then answer the questions that follow.

"What're you doing these holidays?" Spike asked. He lay sprawled upside down on his sleepmat, head hanging over the edge.

Jed was sitting on the floor, scanning through his handscreen, looking for the latest soccer scores.

"I've got a job at the Cosmic Laundry Basket," Jed said, stabbing at the screen.

Spike twisted round to look at him.

"Doing what? Washing and drying? I can't see you doing that!"

Jed grinned. "No, I'm helping with deliveries – they gave me these really cool skins to wear – like a petrol-blue colour, with inbuilt heating controls. Wicked. I'm working with the driver – loading and unloading. You working too?"

"Yup. Waitron on one of Galactron's shuttles."

"No way!"

"Yup, way!" Spike grinned.

"You're kidding. Intergalactic?"

"Nah – you have to be eighteen to serve on those – this is one of the intragalactic ones. It does the Earth-out line – Mars to Pluto."

"Hectic, man. I am so envious!"

And he was. He'd never been Up, although most of his friends had. Actually, that was a lie – he'd been Up once – on a school outing to the Moon, but, then, so had every other 7th grader, so that didn't count, really. The shuttles moved between Earth and the homedomes on the planets. Doing a shuttle trip was one of his dreams – but as his mom said (frequently) – their budget didn't stretch that far – or that high.

"And here I was, so stoked that I had this cool job!"

"Hey, what you're doing is going to be a blast too, man!" Spike was trying to make him feel better. "You get to travel the tunnels, meet new people ..."

"... and deliver their laundry!" Jed finished, with a touch of bitterness. He'd been so proud of the petrol-blue skins, too. Now they just seemed ordinary.

"Come on, let's go dial some snacks to cheer you up."

"Don't mention the Up word," said Jed grumpily. But he pocketed his screen, and followed Spike to the kitchen.

---

a How do you know that this extract is fiction?

_____

b Where do you think the story is set? Give a reason for your answer.

_____

c When do you think this story is set? Quote a line that places the story in the past, the present or the future.

_____

d What do the workers of the Cosmic Laundry Basket do?

_____

e What is Spike doing in his holidays?

_____

f Quote a line to show that Jed is jealous of Spike.

_____

g Rewrite this sentence using indirect speech. Give the sentence a 'speaker'.

"You get to travel the tunnels, meet new people …"

_____

h Write a definition for each of these words from the extract.

sleepmat _____

handscreen _____

skins _____

homedome _____

i What is the difference between 'intergalactic' and 'intragalactic'.

_____

j Where is 'Up'?

_____

k What joke is Jed's mom making when she says, 'their budget didn't stretch that far – or that high'?

_____

2 🎧 Audio 2 Listen to the next extract from the story and answer the questions.

a Which of these adjectives describe Jed's mood? Tick (✓) one answer.

☐ marvellous   ☐ miserable   ☐ manic

b What was Jed's job?

_____

c What figure of speech is 'he steamed like a wet fish'? Tick (✓) one answer.

☐ metaphor ☐ personification ☐ simile

d What is the function of the city dome? Tick (✓) one answer.

☐ It protects the people from acid rain.

☐ It protects the people from ultra-violet light.

☐ It protects the people from predators.

e Rewrite this dialogue into indirect speech.

Droomer: It's lunchtime now, so you can dry out.

Jed: You said that yesterday too. It's not funny.

_____

_____

_____

3 Read this short extract from *A Time Traveller's Guide to the Future*, by I Thomas, then answer the questions.

> ## New types of materials
>
> Different clothes-making techniques meet different needs.
> Synthetic fibres can be melted down and used to form seamless
> garments out of one piece of fabric, perfect for sports gear
> and comfortable pyjamas. People working with chemicals or in
> hospitals can even wear spray-on clothes that are worn once and
> washed off.
>
> > ### Future firsts
> >
> > The world's first spray-on clothes hit the shops
> > in 2011. 'Fabrican' liquid contains thousands of
> > tiny fibres. The liquid evaporates when it is sprayed
> > on to a surface, leaving behind the fibres, which
> > then bind together. Natural or synthetic fibres can
> > be used to create fabrics with different textures.

a What two new types of material have been invented?

_____

_____

b Who would wear each type of material?

_____

_____

c Change each verb to a noun by adding a suffix.

form _____

evaporate _____

contain _____

d Explain how 'Fabrican' works.

_____

_____

e How do you know that this text is fact and not fiction?

_____

f Would you wear spray-on clothes? Explain why or why not.

_____

_____

_____

_____

_____

_____

Write a four-line dialogue between two people, talking about clothes of the future.
Use direct speech, with the correct punctuation.

_____

_____

_____

_____

Look at and think
about each of the
I can statements.

ate: _____

1 Unscramble these words to make simple sentences. Punctuate the sentences correctly.

a private domes the wealthier had people their own

_____

b blue clear skies couldn't remember Jed

_____

c driver the van of he worked Droomer with the

_____

d suit his didn't warm very keep him

_____

e wet fish steamed he like a

_____

2 Add adjectives and adverbs to make these simple sentences more interesting.

a The traveller went to the moon.

_____

b The astronauts watched the view.

_____

c The moon is a satellite.

_____

d Space travel is expensive.

_____

e He has to save money.

_____

3 Choose and circle the correct relative pronoun from the ones in brackets.

a I have a friend (who/which) has been to the rocket launching pad.

b She said it was the best trip (who/that) she had ever taken.

c The entrance ticket, (who/which) she kept, has the NASA logo on it.

d Her parents, (who/which) went with her, were also impressed.

4 Finish these sentences by adding a relative pronoun and additional details.

a The story _____ was very interesting.

_____

b My brother _____ said he would do it again.

_____

c The future _____ is coming closer.

_____

d People _____ might even live longer.

_____

e I know the man _____ very well.

_____

5 Change these verbs to nouns, by adding a suffix.

progress _____

impress _____

televise _____

intrude _____

invade _____

6 Draw lines to match each figure of speech to an example.

a simile	The sun was an egg, sliding over the horizon.
b metaphor	The sea whispered along the shore.
c personification	Full of fury, full of fun
d alliteration	The spaceship descended as fast as lightning.
e idiom	He was all ears when I told him about it.

Look at and think about each of the *I can* statements.

Date: _____

1 You are going to write a story, set in the future. Every story has a conflict of sorts at the centre. The characters, in the setting, solve the conflict.

a Think about a potential conflict. What could be the action at the centre of your story? Make notes here.

_____

_____

_____

_____

b Where is your story set? Make notes here.

_____

_____

_____

_____

c Write a few lines about your characters. What makes them interesting? How do their personalities cope with conflict?

_____

_____

_____

_____

d Think about figurative language. Can you use similes, metaphors, personification or alliteration in your story? Practise writing some here.

_____

_____

_____

_____

e Now look at the graph of a story. Use the graph to help you as you write.

climax

build-up   resolution

introduction   conclusion

2 Write your story here. You should write at least five paragraphs.

_____
_____
_____
_____
_____
_____
_____
_____
_____
_____
_____
_____
_____
_____
_____
_____
_____
_____
_____

3 Improve and edit your writing by using this checklist.

Checklist

- I have followed the plan of the story. ☐

- My characters are interesting. ☐

- I have a clear plot, with a conflict that is solved. ☐

- My setting is well described. ☐

- I have used good examples of figurative language. ☐

Look at and think about each of the *I can* statements. ☐

Date: _____

1 Read this text about snakes, then answer the questions.

Snakes
Subphylum Vertebrata
Class Reptilia
Number of species Over 2,000
Distribution
In warm parts of the world, including the sea, in all habitats.

Prey
A snake can track its prey using its long, forked tongue, which it flicks over the ground. It picks up the smell left by small animals like mice and voles. Some snakes, such as grass snakes, catch their prey by grabbing and swallowing it. Others, such as pythons, coil their bodies around their prey and squeeze it, making it impossible for the animal to breathe. Poisonous snakes attack their prey with their fangs. The poison glands are in the snake's jaw and, as they bite their prey, the poison is injected into its nervous system. Only a third of all the snakes in the world are poisonous.

The black mamba is the fastest snake. It can travel around 15km/hour in short bursts.

a Which of these features make this a factual text? Tick all correct answers.

☐ It uses figurative language.

☐ It has features like headings and captions.

☐ Its purpose is to entertain.

☐ Its purpose is to inform.

b Is the writing style formal or informal? Explain your answer.

_____

c Where would you find text like this? Explain your answer.

_____

d Who would be interested in reading this text? Why do you think this?

_____

e 'Ophidiophobia' means an overwhelming fear of snakes. How do you think a person with this phobia would respond to this text?

_____

f How do you feel about snakes?

_____

2 What type of sentences are these? Write **simple**, **compound** or **complex** under each sentence.

a The black mamba is the fastest snake.

_____

b Snakes are scary to some people, but not all of them are dangerous.

_____

c It tracks its prey using its tongue, which it flicks over the ground.

_____

d They catch their prey by grabbing and swallowing it.

_____

e I'm not scared of snakes, because there are no snakes in New Zealand where I live!

_____

3 Write the connectives in question **2**. Say whether they are coordinate connectives or subordinate connectives.

_____

_____

_____

4 Complete these complex sentences by adding your own subordinate clause. Write the full sentence.

a Some people are afraid of snakes because …

_____

b She is not afraid of snakes, but …

_____

c … it is unwise to keep snakes as pets.

_____

d If I never see a snake again it would be too soon, because …

_____

e I'm interested in looking at snakes, so long as …

_____

Look at and think about each of the _I can_ statements.

Date: _____

1 Read this poem, 'Snake', by Ian Mudie, then answer the questions.

> **Snake**
>
> Suddenly the grass before my feet
> shakes and becomes alive.
> The Snake
> twists, almost leaps
> graceful even in terror,   5
> smoothness looping back over smoothness,
> slithers away, disappears.
> And the grass is still again.
>
> And surely, by whatever means of communication
> is available to Snakes,   10
> the word is passed:
> Hey, I just met a man, a monster too;
> Must have been oh seven feet tall.
> So keep away from the long grass,
> it's dangerous there.   15
>
> *Ian Mudie*

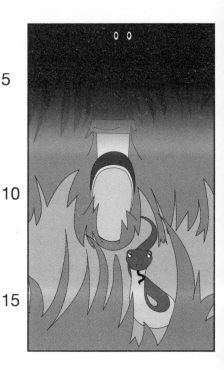

Lines 1–5

a What sound does 'Suddenly … Snake' remind you of?

_____

b What figure of speech is this?

_____

c Does the grass really come alive? Give a reason for your answer.

_____

d What figure of speech is 'the grass comes alive'?

_____

e Find an example of alliteration in lines 4–5.

_____

Lines 6–10

f How many 's' sounds are there in lines 6–10? Write all the words with the 's' sound.

_____

g What does this 's' sound add to the meaning of the poem? Tick (✓) one answer.

☐ It sounds like grass.   ☐ It sounds like a snake hissing.

☐ It sounds like the sea.

Lines 11–15

h Give an example of personification in lines 11–15.

_____

i What do the 'm' sounds add to the meaning of the poem? Tick (✓) one answer.

☐ something not slithery

☐ a big heavy creature arrives

☐ mumbling

j In your opinion, do the 's' and 'm' sounds add to the meaning of the poem?

_____

2 Read these two short fables about snakes, then answer the questions that follow.

The Serpent and the Eagle

A serpent and an eagle were struggling with each other in a deadly conflict. The serpent had the advantage, and was about to strangle the bird. A countryman saw them and, running up, loosed the coil of the serpent and let the eagle go free. The serpent, irritated at the escape of his prey, some time later injected his poison into the drinking cup of the countryman. The rustic, ignorant of his danger, was about to drink, when the eagle struck his hand with his wing and, seizing the drinking cup in his talons, carried it away.

The Fowler and the Viper

A fowler, taking his birdlime and his twigs, went out to catch birds. Seeing a thrush sitting upon a tree, he wished to capture it, and fitting his twigs to a proper length, he watched intently, having his whole thoughts directed towards the sky.

While thus looking upwards, he unawares trod upon a viper asleep, just before his feet. The viper, turning towards him, bit him, and he, falling into a swoon, said to himself: "Woe is me! That while I tried to hunt another, I am myself fallen unawares into the snares of death."

---

a What is similar about these two fables? (Hint: Think about the snakes.)

_____

b Describe the character of the snake in both fables.

_____

c Why do you think snakes are often represented like this in fables?

_____

d What is the moral of each fable?

The Serpent and the Eagle

_____

The Fowler and the Viper

_____

e Write a character list for each fable.

_____

_____

f What is similar about the countryman in each fable?

_____

3 Read these words aloud. Then put them into different columns that show a similar spelling rule for the sound 'k'.

character snake comes kind communication		
conflict countryman coil escape cup capture		
drink carry stomach catch sky cheek		

4 You are going to write your own short fable, featuring Snake, showing his characteristic features.

Remember:

- you need a setting
- you can add more characters
- something needs to happen
- then the problem is solved
- and there's a moral to the fable.

a Plan your fable here.

_____

_____

_____

_____

_____

_____

b Now write your fable out neatly. Check that you have all the elements mentioned in the bullet list at the start of this question.

_____

_____

_____

_____

_____

_____

_____

_____

_____

_____

_____

_____

Look at and think about each of the *I can* statements.

Date: _____

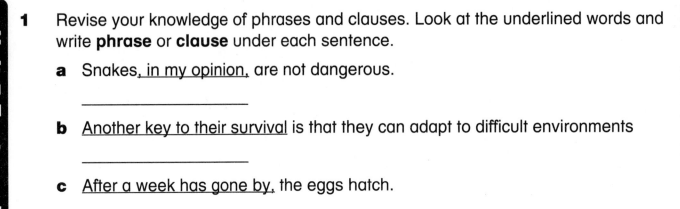

Unit 5 Facts and fables

1 Revise your knowledge of phrases and clauses. Look at the underlined words and write **phrase** or **clause** under each sentence.

a Snakes, in my opinion, are not dangerous.

_____

b Another key to their survival is that they can adapt to difficult environments

_____

c After a week has gone by, the eggs hatch.

_____

d Snakes eat small animals because they need protein.

_____

e The creature is a fly, that looks like a bee.

_____

2 Underline the adverbial clauses and circle the adjectival clauses.

a The black mamba, which you only find in Africa, is the fastest snake.

b Snakes lie on rocks until they warm up in the sun.

c His foot, which was swollen into a grotesque ball, was very painful.

d Write a report that tells me about an animal you like.

3 Use your knowledge of sentences to write a short report about an animal that interests you. Plan your report here. You should plan to include at least one illustration, photograph or chart.

4 Now write your report out neatly. Make sure you have included all the elements in the checklist below.

_____

_____

_____

_____

_____

_____

_____

_____

_____

_____

_____

_____

_____

5 Edit your writing and improve it by using this checklist.

Checklist

My report:

- has a title ☐

- has paragraphs, each with a subheading ☐

- has paragraphs with a clear topic sentence, and supporting sentences ☐

- uses a variety of interesting sentence types ☐

- is written in formal language ☐

- is in the third person ☐

- has diagrams, charts or pictures to support the text. ☐

Look at and think about each of the *I can* statements. ☐

Date: _____

1 Read this extract from *My Journey Across the Indian Ocean* by James Adair, then answer the questions.

The beginning of a crazy idea

I came up with the idea of rowing unsupported across the Indian Ocean when I was living in London with Ben, my best friend from university. We were both struggling in low-paid jobs, and we read in the newspaper about someone who'd rowed across the Pacific Ocean. It just seemed like an amazing thing to do and although we didn't know where to start, we were excited about it straight away.

Starting to dream

Part of my motivation for doing the challenge came from my childhood and becoming seriously ill when I was 14. I developed an illness called Guillain-Barré syndrome, which is a disease of the nervous system. It started a couple of days before I went back to school after the summer holidays. I'd bought some new football boots and was trying to break them in, when I suddenly felt really breathless. The doctor had no idea what was wrong with me, so I went to hospital and within 12 hours of being admitted I was completed paralysed from head to foot – I couldn't see, breathe or speak.

---

a How do you know that this is an autobiography?

_____

b What does the chapter heading 'The beginning of a crazy idea' tell you about how James felt about the adventure?

_____

c Tick (✓) one answer. 'Unsupported' in this text means:

☐ on their own with no help

☐ without a supporting structure

☐ nobody loved them.

d Put these phrases in chronological order.

- although we didn't know where to start   • _____
- when I was living in London with Ben   • _____
- We were excited about it straight away   • _____
- I came up with an idea   • _____

e Which section of this text is a flashback to the past?

_____

f Why do you think the author put in this flashback?

_____

g What system does Guillain-Barré syndrome affect?

_____

h Complete these sentences by adding connectives.

I was trying on some football boots _____ I felt breathless.

_____ the doctor didn't know what was wrong, he sent me

to hospital.

i How do you know that James recovered from this syndrome?

_____

j Write one fact from these two chapters.

_____

k Write one opinion from these two chapters.

_____

2 Read two more short chapters from the book, then answer the questions.

> **Training starts**
>
> After coming up with the idea, Ben and I spent six years planning the trip.
> We had to save up for the boat and prepare ourselves, both physically
> and mentally. A lot of people told us how tough it would be, so I convinced
> myself that it was going to be the worst thing ever, so that, if anything, I'd be
> pleasantly surprised.
>
> Most of the physical training was done in the gym. I cycled to work every day,
> then I'd do two hours in the gym, or swimming. As important as training was
> putting on weight, because we knew we were going to lose a lot. But that was
> the fun bit, just eating mounds of food!
>
> **On our way**
>
> We left at dawn. It was a beautiful morning and the sun was coming up as we
> rowed out of the tiny marina in western Australia.
>
> It took us about ten minutes to reach the open sea, then it just suddenly went
> quiet. We had to navigate some of a shipping lane at the beginning, which was
> quite scary because there were some big ships to get past, but the weather
> was good and we did about 46 kilometres on the first day.

a What reasons does James give for taking six years to get ready for the trip?

_____

_____

b Why did James try to convince himself that 'it was going to be the worst thing ever'?

_____

c Find and write six connectives in the chapter called 'Training starts'.

_____

_____

d Use a connective from part **c** to join these two sentences.

We had to put on weight. We were going to lose a lot.

_____

e How do you think James and Ben feel in the chapter 'On our way'?

_____

f Which adjectives that James uses give clues to how he is feeling?

_____

g Write a sentence with each of these words to show that you know what they mean.

marina: _____

navigate: _____

3 Look at this map of the route that James and Ben took, then answer the question on the next page.

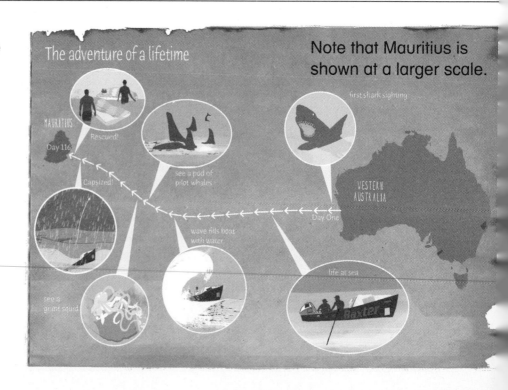

Write a short paragraph to accurately describe their route. Use some of the connectives from the box in your sentences.

first	next	then	after	finally	secondly
	before	later	eventually		

_____

_____

_____

_____

_____

_____

_____

_____

_____

_____

4 Write six sentences of dialogue, between James and Ben, about one of the incidents you can see on the map.

James: _____

_____

Ben: _____

_____

James: _____

_____

Ben: _____

_____

James: _____

_____

Ben: _____

_____

Look at and think about each of the *I can* statements.

Date: _____

1 Imagine you are Ben or James. You are going to give a speech about your rowing trip across the Indian Ocean.

  a Reread the text on the previous pages and study the map.

  b Make notes about what you are going to say. Use this graphic organiser to organise your notes.

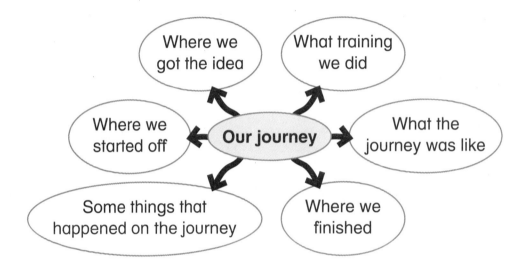

  c Practise your speech and then present it to the class.

2 Join the sentences using connectives from the box. Then write out your new paragraph.

> finally   when   because   but   and

we got to the furthest island.

we really felt like we'd made it

It had been tough

of the currents we'd been rowing hard

only making slow progress.

we were heading out into the expanse of ocean

really on our way.

_____

_____

_____

_____

3 Choose the correct prefix to give each of these adjectives a negative meaning. Then use each word in a sentence, to show you understand what it means.

il-   im-   un-   in-   dis-   mis-

a supported _____

_____

b informed _____

_____

c logical _____

_____

d perfect _____

_____

e happy _____

_____

4 Add a -tch or -ch word from the box to complete each sentence.

patch   stretch   crutch   teach   crouch   fetch   catch

a We were going through a bad _____; everyone was arguing.

b I could never do it; not by any _____ of the imagination!

c She's gone to _____ my sister from school.

d If you _____ a cold, you could stay off school.

e He was walking awkwardly with the _____.

5 Circle the correct connective in each sentence.

a We tried every pattern of rowing (but/because) settled on two hours on, two off.

b We ate at the same time (but/because) we needed company.

c We would stop and eat (because/then) start rowing again.

d (However/But), we ended up taking turns, so one person was always rowing.

e I was coming out of the cabin (but/when) a huge wave hit us.

Look at and think about each of the *I can* statements.

Date: _____

1 Do you know what a kenning poem is? Read this extract from 'My Sister'.

> **My Sister**
>
> Dummy-sucker
> Teddy-thrower
> Anything-chewer
>
> Kiss-giver
> Slave-employer
> Dolly-hugger
> Calm-destroyer

a Write a definition of a kenning poem.

_____

b Look at the topics in the box. Choose one and write a kennings poem about it. Write at least two stanzas.

> the sea   my brother or sister   our house   my family

_____
_____
_____
_____
_____
_____
_____
_____
_____
_____
_____
_____
_____
_____
_____
_____

2   Write a story about an adventure that you have had, with a flashback in it.

The flashback could add extra information about why you went on the adventure, or add something you remember that helps your character.

a   Plan your writing here. Remember, a story has:

- a problem or conflict that needs to be solved
- characters that are involved in the action
- a particular setting.

b   Now write your story here.

_____

_____

_____

_____

c   Check and edit your work.

- Have you got a good introduction?
- Are your characters interesting and well-described?
- Do you have a strong plot (action)?
- Have you included a flashback that helps the action?
- Do you have a good ending?
- Are your spelling and grammar correct?

Look at and think about each of the *I can* statements.

Date: _____

1 Reading and grammar

Read the text below carefully, then answer the questions.

Frozen

No, this is not about the Disney movie. It's about me, literally frozen, on a ledge, on a mountain. I should never have listened to my brother. "A gentle walk," he said. "Fresh air and exercise," he said. What a load of rubbish!

It was a beautiful day, I must grant him that.   5

"Come on, get off the couch," my brother Nate said. "You need some exercise today."

"But, I'm sure I exercised last week," I protested, as he pushed me into my room to put on what he calls 'sensible' shoes.

And so, off we set, on this 'gentle' walk. First, we had to drive to the   10
bottom of a small mountain, then find parking amid a horde of boring-looking people in sensible shoes, with their one hundred dogs and screaming children.

Next was – Nate repeating himself with that word again – a gentle ascent. Within minutes I was puffing. A bunch of rabid walkers pushed past me.   15
We continued in this way for about a half an hour, with me being pushed aside by these keen beans every so often. Soon Nate was so far ahead that I could only see the vague red dot of his beanie.

I finally limped to the top of the hill where Nate was waiting, sitting on a rock and drinking his juice, for all the world like he was in his living   20
room relaxing.

"Look," he said. "Isn't that view beautiful?" My stomach dropped. I froze. I was going to fall off, I just knew it. In kicked my vertigo. Out kicked any common sense.

---

a Why is the title catchy?

_____

b Is this an information text? Give a reason to support your answer.

_____

c What type of text is it?

_____

d Quote a line that shows what the girl thinks of her brother's suggestion.

_____

e Find an uncountable noun in line 6.

_____

f Rewrite these sentences in indirect speech.

"You need some exercise today."

_____

"But I'm sure I exercised last week," I protested.

_____

g Why does the writer put the word 'gentle' in quotation marks?

_____

_____

h Write two connectives in lines 8–11.

_____

_____

i What can you infer about the writer's opinion of walkers from this phrase?

a horde of boring-looking people in sensible shoes, with their one hundred dogs and screaming children

_____

_____

_____

_____

_____

_____

_____

j Write a synonym for each word.

gentle	
ascent	
keen	
relaxed	

k Acrophobia is a fear of heights. Find a word in the last paragraph that has a similar meaning.

_____

2   Reading

Read this text, then answer the questions.

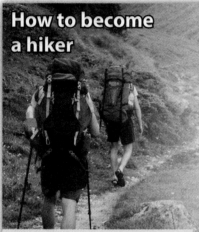

How to become a hiker

Always hike with someone else, and carry food, water, extra clothing and a mobile phone with you.

1. Get fit

You will have a miserable time if you are unfit. Start by walking for half an hour every day. Gradually increase the distance and the time you walk. Vary the incline – hill work is important in building stamina.

2. Hike with a friend

Always hike with someone else. There is safety in numbers. If one of you falls, the other can help. If you get lost, you have company until you are found – which leads me to point number three.

3. Be prepared

Carry a mobile phone with you, and make sure that someone at home knows where you are. You need to take water with you, and snack food with a high energy content. Throw in an extra cereal bar too, in case you need to wait for a rain storm to pass, or wait to be rescued. Always have enough warm clothes with you. Pack an extra layer in case you get wet.

a   Write three things that show that this is an information text.

_____

_____

_____

b   Find an adverbial clause of manner in the first sentence in paragraph 1.

_____

c   What is the function of the dash in the first paragraph?

_____

d   What type of sentence is this?

Throw in an extra cereal bar too, in case you need to wait for a rain storm to pass, or wait to be rescued.

_____

e   Write a proverb from paragraph 2.

_____

f   Find an adjectival phrase in paragraph 3.

_____

g   What important aspects of hiking does the caption show?

_____

3   Writing

a   Write a set of guidelines for a beginner about one of these topics:

- how to prepare to play a sport
- how to survive your first day at school
- how to make or do your favourite thing.

b   Plan your writing here. Remember that your information text:

- should have headings
- will use connectives to join sentences and paragraphs
- should have a mix of different sentence types
- will include one illustration with a caption.

_____

_____

_____

_____

_____

c   Write your text out neatly here.

Look at and think about each of the *I can* statements.

Date: _____

1 Read these pages from the book *What if we run out of oil?* by Nick Hunter, then answer the questions.

How much oil do we use?

There are seven billion people in the world today and between us we use 30 billion **barrels** of oil each year. That's nearly five barrels of oil per year for every man, woman, and child on the planet.

That's an awful lot of oil, but the amount of oil we use is actually growing. This is partly because countries like China and India are becoming richer. As people get richer, they want to travel more and buy cars and many other things that use a lot of oil, such as televisions, computers, **disposable** goods and packaged food.

Not everyone uses a lot of oil. In **developing countries**, many people use wood as fuel for cooking, and travel on foot. They live without oil every day. They use more local, natural materials and grow their own food. The biggest users of oil are still **developed countries** like the countries of western Europe, the USA and Australia.

Country	How much oil do they use in a year?
USA	25 barrels per person
Australia	17 barrels per person
UK	11 barrels per person
China	2 barrels per person
India	1 barrel per person
Bangladesh	1 barrel for every 5 people
Chad, Central Africa	1 barrel for every 20 people

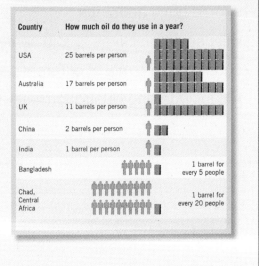

a How do you know that this is an information text?

_____

b What do you think the writer believes about how much oil we use?

_____

c Quote one sentence from the text to support your answer to part **b**.

_____

d Explain the difference in oil use between developing countries and developed countries.

_____

e How do you think the developed countries got 'developed'?

_____

f Write four facts that the infographic gives.

_____

_____

_____

_____

2 Read these two people's opinions about oil use today.

Oil is essential in our lives. It's not only that we need oil to drive cars and run vital machinery, like life support systems in hospitals; we use oil in everything! There is oil in your toothpaste, and in your hair conditioner. Plastics are made with oil. How can you even suggest that we reduce our oil usage? It's irresponsible! If we use 25 barrels of oil a day per person, that's our business, not the rest of the world's.

You're taking this personally. I'm not targeting the USA when I say we need to reduce our reliance on oil. I'm talking about all of us. Look around you. Have you not seen what's happening to the weather around the world? Burning oil to provide energy has destroyed our climate system. Just this week Europe and America are battling intense heatwaves with people dying, while in southern Africa temperatures have dropped so far that it is snowing in Johannesburg! We have got to find alternative forms of energy, and we have got to do this immediately. Now!

a List all the uses of oil that the man mentions.

_____

_____

_____

b How does he try to appeal to your emotions?

_____

c Write a rhetorical question from his speech.

_____

d Give one example of his own opinion.

_____

e Why do you think he is so angry?

_____

_____

f What main example does the woman give for reducing oil use?

_____

g Give an example of a rhetorical question from her speech.

_____

h How does she appeal to your emotions?

_____

i Write an example of repetition from the woman's speech.

_____

j Who do you agree with more? Give a reason for your answer.

_____

_____

3 Here is another infographic from the book _What if we run out of oil?_

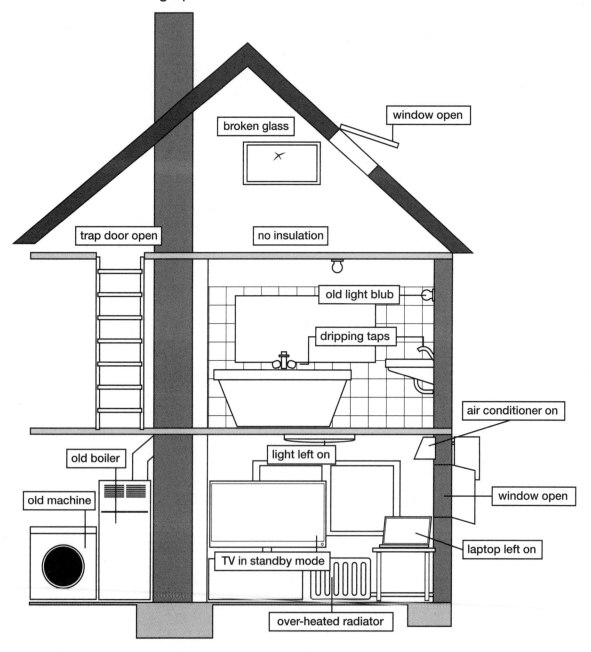

a What is an 'infographic'?

_____

b Give this infographic a title.

_____

c Which of the ideas do you think you could apply in your home?

_____

d Why might this infographic not be very useful in a developing country?

_____

e Design your own infographic on this topic, for the area you live in.

4 Read this extract.

Persuasive texts

Persuasive texts are:

- non-fiction
- one-sided
- intended to convince the reader that the viewpoint being presented is the correct one.

Choose one of the viewpoints in question **2**. Write a paragraph to explain how the person's speech meets the criteria for persuasive texts.

_____

_____

_____

_____

_____

Look at and think about each of the *I can* statements.

Date: _____

1 Fill in the missing semicolons in these sentences.

a Oil is found in oil fields these are large oil-rich areas.

b Pollution is increasing the temperature of the planet this leads to more fires, floods and heatwaves.

c Delegates attending the climate conference were from: Nairobi, Kenya Paris, France and Madrid, Spain.

d Activists struck again last night however, the police prevented them from spray-painting the building again.

e Our oil reserves are declining they need to be protected.

2 Fill in the missing colons in these sentences.

a Pack the following for the protest march a mask, a bottle of water and your placard.

b There is only one solution stop using oil.

c The protest starts at 12 30 on the dot.

d This is what I know all of us will suffer if the climate breaks down.

e These are the people in our group James, Becky, Niraj and Steve.

3 **a** Underline all the verbs in this passage.

The Earth's temperature is rising. This is causing extreme weather events, such as floods and droughts. Most scientists believe that our appetite for burning fossil fuels including coal, oil and gas is actually changing Earth's climate. This is because burning fossil fuels produces a gas called **carbon dioxide**. The amount of this gas in Earth's atmosphere has increased by about one third in the last 250 years.

b Now make two lists: one of all the action verbs in the passage, and one of all the linking verbs.

_____

_____

_____

_____

_____

_____

4 Learn to spell these words with 'j'. Use each word in a sentence to show you know what it means.

adjust

adjourn

adjective

prejudice

project

_____

_____

_____

_____

_____

_____

_____

_____

_____

_____

_____

_____

Look at and think about each of the *I can* statements.

Date: _____

1 Use this template to plan a balanced argument on one of these topics:

- Stop oil use now.
- Legalise rhino poaching.
- All zoos should be closed.

Introduction – a short explanation of the topic	
Paragraph 1 – argument supported by viewpoint	
Paragraph 2 Another argument – supported by viewpoint	
Third argument – supported by viewpoint	
Conclusion – sum up the arguments and give your opinion	

2   Now write out your balanced argument neatly here.

_____

_____

_____

_____

_____

_____

_____

_____

_____

_____

_____

_____

_____

_____

_____

_____

_____

_____

_____

_____

_____

Remember

Each argument should have a main topic sentence, and supporting sentences backing up that viewpoint.

Look at and think about each of the _I can_ statements.

Date: _____

Unit 8 I spy

1 Read this extract from *The World's First Women Doctors*, by Isabel Thomas, then answer the questions.

A World Without Women

Two hundred years ago, the world of medicine was a very strange place:

- Doctors treated patients by letting leeches suck their blood!

- Few people believed that germs caused disease!

- Women were not allowed to be doctors!

Just before Queen Victoria came to the throne, two girls were born who would change medicine forever. Elizabeth Blackwell and Elizabeth Garrett Anderson grew up 3,500 miles and 15 years apart. But they shared the same goal: to train as doctors.

At the time, this seemed impossible. Most people believed that women's brains and bodies were too weak to learn about medicine. Blackwell and Garrett Anderson set out to prove the world wrong.

The Battle Begins

Elizabeth Blackwell began her journey in America in 1844. She wrote to doctors and medical schools to ask how a woman could train as a doctor.

Each time she got the same reply: "It's impossible." One said that Blackwell would only be able to study medicine if she disguised herself as a man! Blackwell did not give up. She began working as a teacher to save money for her training. In her spare time, she read medical books and took private lessons.

Blackwell's lucky break came when she applied to Geneva College in New York. The head of the college felt bad about turning her down without a good reason, so he decided to let the students vote. The students thought it would be funny to say yes, and Blackwell got the acceptance letter she'd been waiting three years for.

In November 1847, Blackwell began life as a student doctor.

> **Mini-biography:**
> **Margaret Bulkley** (1795–1865)
>
> Margaret Bulkley disguised herself as a man for 46 years, so she could train and work as a doctor in the early 1800s. 'James Barry' had a reputation for being a fierce but very good doctor, and even became a hospital inspector. The truth was only discovered when 'James' died.

a Which features of this text show that it is an information text?

_____

b What figurative language is used in the heading 'A World Without Women'?

_____

c Find another use of this type of figurative language.

_____

d What do you find most strange about how medicine was practised 200 years ago?

_____

e Put this passive sentence into active voice.

Women were not allowed to be doctors.

_____

f What did Blackwell and Garrett Anderson set out to prove?

_____

g How would you have replied to Blackwell then? And today?

_____

h What is the difference between a biography and an autobiography?

_____

i Who was 'James Barry'?

_____

j Why is the text about James Barry set in its own block?

_____

2 Read this infographic from the same book, then answer the questions.

FEELING TRAPPED

As teenagers, both Elizabeth Blackwell and Elizabeth Garrett Anderson began to worry about the next stage of their lives. They didn't feel excited about the 'normal' path ahead.

THE EXPECTED PATHS IN THE 1800S

Boy	Girl
school education	learn sewing and music at home
↓	↓
university education	learn perfect manners
↓	↓
choose a profession	
↓	
get married and have children, but never do housework or childcare	get married and have children
↓	↓
spend each day at work	spend each day sitting in the drawing room, or looking after children and home
↓	↓
share your opinions in conversations	keep your opinions to yourself, unless talking about children and home

a What is this type of infographic called? Tick (✓) one answer.

☐ a spider diagram

☐ a graph

☐ a flow chart

b Do you think the 'expected path' for girls has changed? Draw your own flow chart to show what the path for girls looks like now.

c Do you agree with the 'expected path' for boys in the 1800s? Redraw the path to show other options, after 'school education'. You may want to use a spider diagram, instead of a flow chart.

3 Read this paragraph. Write the correct past tense form of the verbs in brackets.

During the 12th century, many new universities _____ (to open) in Europe. From then on, only people who _____ (to study) medicine at university _____ (to be allowed) to call themselves doctors, and women _____ (to be banned) from universities.

Women _____ (to begin) working as nurses in hospitals during the 11th century, but during the Middle Ages, conditions _____ (to be) terrible, and nursing _____ (to be seen) as a job for women who _____ (to have) no other choices. Things _____ (to begin) to improve in the 1600s and 1700s, and some women _____ (to use) their roles as nurses or midwives to make important improvements in healthcare.

4 Write a suitable heading for the paragraph in question **3**.

_____

Look at and think about each of the *I can* statements.

Date: _____

1 Correct the meaning of this paragraph, by adding prefixes from the box to the words in bold. Rewrite the paragraph correctly below.

> un-   dis-   im-   fe-   wo-

Many **men** were **qualified** from learning to be a doctor because they were **male**. It was almost **possible** to get training. **Fortunately**, people thought **men** were **suited** to medicine because their brains and bodies were too weak. This was later **proved**.

_____

_____

_____

_____

2 Change these sentences from passive into active voice.

a Women were not allowed to work as doctors.

_____

b It was believed that they were not suited to study medicine.

_____

c This was proved wrong in later years.

_____

d A protest is being held about the working conditions.

_____

3 Change these sentences from active into passive voice.

a The female doctor wrote the story of her life.

_____

b Many people have signed a petition in support of them.

_____

c The government is helping the students.

_____

4 Read the letter on the next page from a trainee nurse to his parents. Correct the spelling and language errors on the letter itself. Change informal words to more standard English words.

Dear Mum and Dad

Well, I finaly got here and jeepers, what a place! Its absolutely huge. The college is this brick place with fancy columns like you see on the telly, I kid you not! The dormitorys are more my style – like those flats we staid in when I was a kid – you now, the ones with the balconys?

Anyhoo its really nice and I share a room with the only other bloke. Getting a bit tyred of the jokes about mail nurses to be honest. I mean people should of got used to this by now. I mean this is 2023 innit?

But everyone's really friendly and im gonna have a blast.

Theirs not much more to say.

Love two all and see you soon

Billy xxx

5   Put these sentences into the future tense.

a   The community college is opening on Saturday.

_____

b   People come from all over to enjoy the celebration.

_____

c   We are waiting patiently in the queue.

_____

d   New doctors are graduating today.

_____

Look at and think about each of the *I can* statements.

Date: _____

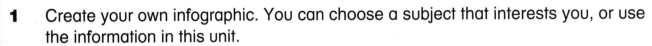

1 Create your own infographic. You can choose a subject that interests you, or use the information in this unit.

- Use a flow chart, a spider diagram, a graph, or any other graphic organiser to present your information.

- Pictures or photographs should have a caption.

- Remember to give your infographic a title.

2 Write a letter or an email to a friend telling them about some of the new things you have learned this week – in school or outside of school. Remember to use the correct format for your letter or email. You need:

- an address
- a greeting
- three to four paragraphs
- a line between each paragraph
- a farewell.

_____

_____

_____

_____

_____

_____

_____

_____

_____

_____

_____

_____

_____

_____

_____

_____

_____

_____

_____

_____

Look at and think about each of the _I can_ statements.

Date: _____

1  Listen to this extract from a school play.
As you listen, complete this table.

Thwarted by Love:
A play in Two Acts

Written by Chris Colte,
Andi Lomboli and Busi Majoja

Setting:		
What do we know about Andi?	**What do we know about Busi?**	**What do we know about Chris?**

2 Read the next scene of the play.

Act One Scene Two

The same table at the canteen, several hours later. Crumpled up paper shows evidence of some frustrated writing attempts.

CHRIS: Thwarted, that's what I am! This whole idea has thwarted me.

ANDI: *(laughing as she picks up and uncrumples some paper)*

Let's see what you've written here.

(He lunges for the paper, which she holds out of reach as she reads.)

'Your eyes are as blue as my football shorts.' Oh my goodness Chris, you're a poet!

(She turns the paper over and reads the other side.)

'You are my heart, let's run away together.'

(ANDI and BUSI burst out laughing; CHRIS looks offended.)

CHRIS: At least I'm trying!

BUSI: Sorry, Chris. You're right. You are a terribly terrific trier of note!

a Where is this scene set?

_____

b Who are the characters?

_____

c What punctuation is used for dialogue?

_____

d Where and how are the characters' names written?

_____

e Why is it important for an actor to take note of stage directions?

_____

3 Answer these questions about the language of the playscript.

a Find a simile in the script.

_____

b Do you think it is a good simile? Explain why or why not.

_____

c What figure of speech is 'You are my heart'?

_____

d Quote an example of alliteration from the script.

_____

e Write your own definition of the word 'thwarted'.

_____

4 Explain the tone of voice of each of the characters. Choose two words from the box for each character.

| teasing | hurt | comforting | offended | conciliatory | mocking |

_____

_____

_____

_____

Look at and think about each of the _I can_ statements.

Date: _____

1 Rewrite each sentence using the correct form of the verb in brackets.

  a Yesterday I (to watch) the play at school.

  _____

  b I (to look) forward to it and I (to be) not disappointed!

  _____

  c Tomorrow, I (to hike) up the mountain; I (to need) to dress warmly as it (to be) going to be cold!

  _____

  _____

  d Everything (to feel) strange today; the weather (to be) weird, with warm wind that (to blow).

  _____

  _____

2 Make these simple sentences complex by adding a subordinate clause.

  a We have to write a play.

  _____

  b We're supposed to use our imagination.

  _____

  c I have already finished my work.

  _____

  d Your writing is interesting.

  _____

3 One of the words in each list of synonyms does not belong. Circle the odd word in each set.

  a strange   unusual   bizarre   boring   odd

  b restful   unhappy   sad   depressed

  c colourful   wan   bright   iridescent

  d lively   alert   slow   busy   energetic

4   Write one of your own examples of each of these figures of speech.

   a   metaphor

   _____

   b   simile

   _____

   c   alliteration

   _____

   d   onomatopoeia

   _____

5   Change these adjectives to nouns.

   a   peaceful _____

   b   happy_____

   c   excited_____

   d   fearful_____

   e   cowardly_____

6   Change these words into verbs.

   a   simple _____

   b   performance _____

   c   pretence _____

   d   lovely _____

   e   revolution _____

7   Write a complex sentence to show what each character was thinking.

   Andi _____

   _____

   Busi _____

   _____

   Chris _____

   _____

Look at and think
about each of the
I can statements.

Date: _____

1 Write the next scene in the play *Thwarted by Love* starring Chris, Andi and Busi. What will happen next? Write a full scene.

_____

_____

_____

_____

_____

_____

_____

_____

_____

2 Use this checklist to improve and edit your work.

Checklist

• My script has a setting. ☐

• Stage directions are in the present tense and in brackets. ☐

• Characters' names are written on the left and followed by a colon. ☐

• Each speaker starts on a new line. ☐

• There are no speech marks. ☐

• I have used some imaginative figurative language. ☐

---

3 Practise reading your playscript aloud with your group.

Try to take on the character you are reading.

• What do they look like and sound like?

• What mannerisms do they have?

• Vary your pace.

• Speak clearly and project your voice, so that others can hear you.

4 Now read your script to the class.

Who has the most interesting scene?

You could vote on this as a class.

5 Write a review of one of the scenes. Use this template.

Name of the scene:

Writers:

Star rating out of five: ☆ ☆ ☆ ☆ ☆

I liked this scene because …

The type of people who will enjoy watching this are …

I would recommend watching this because …

Date: _____

Look at and think about each of the *I can* statements.

1 Read this poem, then answer the questions.

> **My instructions**
>
> "Write a poem," they said,
> "And use some poetic devices."
> My purple pen penned this poem.
> I hope that suffices?
>
> "No need to be cheeky," they said,
> "Just use some rhyme and stuff."
> I rhyme in time, sublime.
> I hope that's enough?
>
> *Fiona Macgregor*

a Describe the attitude of the poet.

_____

_____

_____

_____

b Write down one word that explains what 'they' think about the poet.

_____

c Find an example of alliteration in the poem.

_____

d Which two phrases repeat in the poem? What is the effect of the repetition?

_____

_____

_____

_____

e Write down the rhyming words in the poem.

_____

_____

_____

_____

f Give an example of internal rhyme.

_____

2 Grammar, spelling and punctuation

Read the text, then answer the questions.

How long will it last?

There are different views about how much oil we have left. Oil is not likely to run out next week. If we keep using the same amount of oil as we use now, there is enough oil already discovered to last for 50 years. If we continue to use more oil every year, it won't last as long.

Did you know?

Use of oil in developing countries is likely to increase 2.5 times by 2020. Worldwide demand for electricity to power things such as televisions and computers will increase by 70% over the same period. Many countries produce the electricity they need using power stations that burn oil.

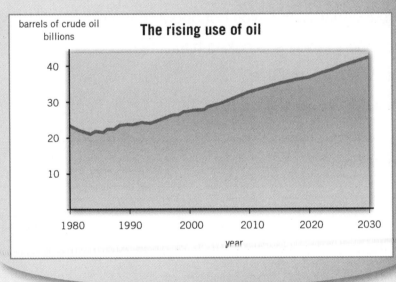

a Identify two linking verbs in the text.

_____

b Write an example of the use of the future tense.

_____

c What type of sentence is the first sentence? Tick (✓) one answer.

☐ compound   ☐ complex   ☐ simple

d Write a synonym for each word.

discover _____

produce _____

e Write two adjectives from this sentence.

Many countries produce electricity from large power stations that burn oil.

_____

f Write two facts from the infographic (not from the text above it).

_____

_____

3 **Grammar, spelling and punctuation**

a Underline the subordinate clause in each sentence.

- The thing that I don't understand is where she got the idea from.
- I saw that woman who presents the environment show on TV at the shops on Saturday.

b Punctuate these sentences correctly.

- We finally came to a conclusion it was not about money.
- Where did you go to yesterday she asked him.

c Join these sentences with a connective.

- I had to leave early. My exam started at eight.

_____

d Write a fact and an opinion.

Fact:_____

Opinion:_____

e Change the verbs in these sentences into the tenses in brackets.

- He is training when they arrived. (past continuous)

_____

- She took it out of the oven. (future perfect tense)

_____

- We ate our meal as quickly as possible. (present continuous)

_____

4 Writing

Write a persuasive argument on one of the topics below. You can argue the topic from any perspective.

Remember:

- you need a strong opening paragraph and conclusion
- you should back up your argument with at least three points.

Using oil is essential for the survival of the human race.

All cities should have a car-free zone.

Poetry should be compulsory in schools.

It's time to throw art out of the curriculum and make every person learn science.

_____

_____

_____

_____

_____

_____

_____

_____

_____

_____

_____

_____

_____

_____

_____

_____

_____

_____

_____

Look at and think about each of the *I can* statements.

Date: _____

Acknowledgements

Text acknowledgements
The publishers gratefully acknowledge the permission granted to reproduce the copyright material in this book. Every effort has been made to trace copyright holders and to obtain their permission for the use of copyright material. The publishers will gladly receive any information enabling them to rectify any error or omission at the first opportunity.

We are grateful to the following for permission to reproduce copyright material:

Cover illustration: *Hall of the Bulls* Reprinted by permission of HarperCollins*Publishers* Ltd © 2014 Tom Bradman, illustrated by Nicholas Jackson; *The Railway Children* Reprinted by permission of HarperCollins*Publishers* Ltd © 2016 Harriet Castor, illustrated by Rosalind Lyons; *Hall of the Bulls* Reprinted by permission of HarperCollins*Publishers* Ltd © 2014 Tom Bradman, illustrated by Nicholas Jackson; *The Porridge Pincher* Reprinted by permission of HarperCollins*Publishers* Ltd © 2012 David Wood, illustrated by Tom Percival; The poem on p.28, "Gran, can you rap?" by Jack Ousbey, copyright © Jack Ousbey. Reproduced by kind permission; *All About Me* Reprinted by permission of HarperCollins*Publishers* Ltd © 2009 Michael Rosen; An extract on p.38 from *I am Malala: The Girl Who Stood Up for Education and Was Shot by the Taliban* by Malala Yousafzai, with Christina Lamb, Weidenfeld & Nicholson an imprint of Orion Publishing Group Ltd, 2013, copyright © 2013. Reproduced by permission of Orion through PLSClear; and Little, Brown and Company an imprint of Hachette Book Group, Inc; *A Time Traveller's Guide to the Future* Reprinted by permission of HarperCollins*Publishers* Ltd © 2012 Isabel Thomas; The Poem on p.52 "Snake" by Ian Mudie, https://allpoetry.com/poem/8522217-Snake-by-Ian-Mudie. Reproduced by kind permission of the family of the late Ian Mudie; *My Journey Across the Indian Ocean* Reprinted by permission of HarperCollins*Publishers* Ltd © 2013 James Adair, illustrated by Joey Marsh; The Kennings poem on p.64 "My Sister", https://www.youngwriters.co.uk/types-kennings, copyright © Young Writers (Part of Bonacia Ltd). Reproduced by permission; *What if we run out of oil?* Reprinted by permission of HarperCollins*Publishers* Ltd © 2012 Nick Hunter; *The World's First Women Doctors* Reprinted by permission of HarperCollins*Publishers* Ltd © 2015 Isabel Thomas.

Photo acknowledgements
The publishers gratefully acknowledge the permission granted to reproduce the copyright material in this book. Every effort has been made to trace copyright holders and to obtain their permission for the use of copyright material. The publishers will gladly receive any information enabling them to rectify any error or omission at the first opportunity.

P27 Jason Stitt/Shutterstock; p40 Deni_Sugandi/Shutterstock; p44 National News/TopFoto; p50 Cormac Price; p68 Dzmitrock/Shutterstock; Design Pics Inc/Alamy Stock Photo; p74 agefotostock/Alamy Stock Photo; p79 Alpha Stock/Alamy Stock Photo.